Author Details

Geraldine Taylor is Educational Consultant to Penguin's birth to eight publishing team, and a counsellor for students at Bristol University.

She is a multi-award winning author and was BBC Wildlife Writer of the Year in 2000.

with warmest wishes, Geraldine Taylor

Echo lands

and other true tales of the Avon Gorge Woods

Geraldine Taylor

EYE ON Books,
Bristol

Echo lands

First published 2006

Author: Geraldine Taylor
Published by: EYE ON Books
Editor: Peter Taylor
Design: Keith Taylor
Text Illustrations: by kind permission
of Robin Tanner

Cover & other Illustrations: Sandra Moore
Mob: 07812 058947
sandrad.moore@virgin.net
www.sandradmoore.com

Production: Competitive Colour Print
6 Hartington Park, Redland, Bristol BS6 7ES
Tel: 0117 924 3388 Fax: 0117 924 1155
Email: ccp@issuk.co.uk
Web: www.issuk.co.uk

ISBN-13 978-0-9551823-0-3
ISBN-10 0-9551823-0-1

Eye On Books
28, Berkeley Road Bristol, BS6 7PJ
0117-973-2787
eyeon.books@virgin.net

Foreword

It begins always with the smallest of details. Something fragile, overlooked, diffident: two bluebells in a single-belled flower; the colours of a nuthatch lit by a rainbow; the outrage in a blackcap's alarm call. Geraldine Taylor wanders through her springtime woods in Avon Gorge reduced to the size of "the seed leaves of herb Robert". Everything in this world of huge and universal significance commands not just her attention but her respect. She apologises to the blackcap and begins singing the Handel's *hallelujah chorus*. Of course, everything joins in. "Today", she writes, "I'm just part of the business of the woods".

But this isn't prissy, self-conscious writing. Her diary is full of festive, raucous, self-mocking passages. Its unapologetic, tip-toed excitement reminds me of Annie Dillard: what would one ever do, walking in the springtime, but gasp ("Fantastic! Fantastic!"), sing, nod to nuthatches, sit down with a deer or a yew tree, join in with the whole fizzing party? And, of course, when you come across a woman dipping her hair, perfectly naturally, in a rainwater puddle, it isn't "a pagan ritual or a romantic spell" but the aftermath of a more wondrously earthy contact : "A bird shat on my head". It's just part of the business of the woods – a business which, through Geraldine Taylor's eyes, has the exaltation and comedy and real equality of love.

Richard Mabey

Author of Flora Britannica

The Woodland floor in early Spring

For Keith,
who makes
everything possible,
for Peter
whose robin spirit
flies with me;
and to the memory
of the late, great
Robin and
Heather Tanner,
and Dietrich Hanff.

Also Derwent May,
writer and Times nature diarist,
who has encouraged
EYE ON Magazine
from the beginning.

GT

Echo lands,
and other true tales of the Avon Gorge Woods.

Woodlanders

I'll be a bird listener today, content with the song and the shadow …

March 28th 7.20 am

Deer on my mind: I know I'm first here because I'm breaking spider ropes slung across the path, I can feel them on my nose. I'm so quiet that I can't hear my own footfalls. Even so, my presence is rapidly announced …

One of the jays (high-handed gatekeepers of the woods) shrieks *off-with-her-head,* and a fat wood pigeon rockets out of the ivy. In the kafuffle, three deer bound down the wooded slope of the Gorge. They *knew* I was there even though I had no idea they were close. How am I to become a seasoned deer watcher if they bounce off in a flurry of fluffed-up white bottoms every time I arrive?

Today, I'm leaving my binoculars in the rucksack. I wear them as identity – *It's OK for me to lurk around in woods, see, I'm a birdwatcher* … I have this need to explain myself. Yesterday, I tumbled in the mud. Sitting there, my first prim act was to reinstate my binoculars so that anyone chancing by would realise that I was a toppled birdwatcher, not a fallen woman.

My most interesting encounter with this need to explain was in these woods a while ago. I came across a lady dipping her hair in the rainwater that had collected in a semi-hollow tree. A pagan ritual? A romantic spell? I contained my curiosity but she rushed to confound my theorising by explaining that *a bird shat on my head.*

I use binoculars to see hunters (peregrines, sparrow hawks, buzzards and kestrels) and woodpeckers, but other woodland birds come closer when I'm without them. This tree creeper scuttles up the trunk in front of me and I can even see its darning-needle beak. And maybe I don't always need to see. Often getting a better view means disturbing*: I'll be a bird *listener* today, content with the song and the shadow.

Here are two bluebells in single-belled flowers like little blue railway signals, six cut-paper anemones, and wood violets snuggling at the base of the trees. Something makes me turn and there, about an eighth of a mile away, maybe more, I can see another woodlander. I didn't consciously hear him, certainly didn't smell him but something told me that I wasn't alone. If I can sense this, then it's no wonder that the deer know I've arrived.

* Having been told off by an outraged blackcap (a rare event, as these warblers sing from cover and don't

Bastard Balm and Cuckoo-pint

usually show themselves), I would never again risk getting too close for the sake of seeing more clearly. The bird's *tuts* had all the remembered disappointment and frustration of a parental scolding.

Celebrity worship – (a fragment)

There are certain woodland birds I don't bother to binocular. This is like saying I don't get out of bed for a blue tit and yet, through the lense, there's no bird as heart-breakingly pretty. I'm also guilty of inflation, telling those who ask, about peregrines, buzzards, ravens and woodpeckers, as though only celebrity sightings will claim attention – but all the while my heart is with the woodland birds. It's time to talk about blue tits and robins again.

Alice

I meander around the woods avoiding notices

I guess I've told everyone that I was in the woods on the day the bull escaped, the bull that made the National News and turned out to be called *George*. But something far more important happened to me that day.

I was lured to Leigh Woods early in the year and at dawn by the hope of sunbeams through leaf-bare trees. Only sporadic birdsong and the bony knockings of branches in the wind broke the dreamy silence, and on I walked …

I wandered into the forest, looking for the badger sett by the cowslip (and finding it again but not yet the cowslip) and then on and on until I came face to face with a notice, on pink cardboard:

BEWARE
BULL LOOSE IN WOODS
DANGEROUS ANIMAL
DO NOT APPROACH   if seen, telephone ....

Why, I wondered, is the notice *pink*? In the hope of attracting the bull perhaps, like moths to a lamp, or butterflies to the colour white. Also I was cross that there was a notice at all on this remote pathway: I meander around woods avoiding notices. Information boards about wildlife tend to be smug and I don't want to be welcomed here in writing. It spoils the discovery, my first-person-here-since-the-beginning-of-time imaginings. After all, Rat and Mole didn't listen, awestruck, to the Piper at the Gates of Dawn under a *National Trust* notice telling them the salient features of the place.

I didn't change my pace or direction (both came later, along with fear). The sun shone its torch into a tunnel of catkins and primrose buds and, obediently, I entered. Two male blackbirds criss-crossed the path in their important-things-to-do way and then a mousy creature sped across in the slipstream of a blackbird and squeezed through a hole in the base of a tree stump. I kept sight of the hole and sat on the stump. I was examining the seed leaves of herb Robert when the mouse came back, sat in a leafy scoop beside the stump and stared at me with intensely dark eyes. It was a bank vole and it had come back.

My rabbit Lucy behaved like this when I brought her home from the pet shop. Whenever I looked in her hutch she'd make a fuss of bolting into the private area and then, seconds later, she'd creep out again to look at me.

So there we were down our *Alice in Wonderland* tunnel – me and the fat little bank vole, and, somewhere else in the forest, the darkly funny threat of a runaway bull.

Perching (another fragment)

I'm territorial, like birds: I've had the same perch at work for eleven years. As a therapist, I should challenge myself for this rigidity, but birds don't ponder on the roots of their behaviour.

I'm searching the woods for a perch, a place to make for and to settle on every time I'm here. Like nesting wrens, I'll try several set-ups before I make my selection. I need a mossy stump, songs from a warbler, and the warm companionship of a yew.

Echo lands

As choir leader, I nod in the direction of the nuthatch next to call.

Wood Anemone

Nuthatches are snappy dressers: these plump peach and grey birds have much of the dandy of the green woodpecker, and a lot of the *quick-look!* rarity of the kingfisher. Not that they are rare here: here they *own* the place and I see more nuthatches than robins. If you've never seen a nuthatch, and lots of people tell me they would love to, then come here, stare at tree trunks when the sun is on them and it won't take long.

I'm listening to the nuthatch's fruity call, *I'm here, here, here* and there's a one-second silence before other nuthatches echo their answers from all points of the compass. In order to hear them, though, I must disregard competing choirs of thrushes and great tits and the thrilling drumming of the great spotted woodpeckers.

In the reserve at Ashton Court, I heard five willow warblers calling and answering in an order I could predict, and sometimes overlapping like a round. I'm listening to see if the nuthatches reply in predictable order, and as choir leader, I nod in the direction of the nuthatch next to call.

Of course, if I were listening under a more distant tree, the nuthatch *there* would be the lead caller, and the bird above me now would be one of those answering so urgently, proclaiming its right to territory. Let's see if I can navigate to one of the distant birds to get an idea of how much personal space nuthatches need. This is why I'm picking my way between nuthatches, careful not to tread on the first bluebells, here in Echo lands.

4th April

Frost

This is no time to obey the rules ...

Something astonishing can happen when there's frost in April. I'm racing into the woods at seven, crunching over white grass, and tiptoeing up the banks of the ancient encampment to perch on top of the world.

This rainbow light *lives,* electrifies. The air amplifies each note of birdsong and I see feathers bright with spangles. The nuthatch is a pearl; the robin's chest luminous orange and the blue tits sparkle like mimosa. That jaggedly cut branch on the ash trunk could be a great spotted woodpecker, and, as I wonder, that's what it becomes and it flies off, red as blood. On the paths, dried beech leaves shuffle, form into coal tits and chaffinches, and then, mysteriously, turn back again into leaves. A heron rows across the clear blue ocean and no other bird soars up to challenge it. There's even a lilt in the call of the chiff-chaff as though this is no time to obey the rules.

The spell breaks now, and by the tiniest hardening of the light. The day moves out of the crystal, moves on, or perhaps begins. There's warmth in the sun. I didn't need to pinch myself to make sure it was real because the tree stump I sat on was surrounded by vicious new nettles ... For a while though, and it will happen again, God was with me, and the world was mine.

9th April

Fire eyes ... *(a fragment)*

Why are the woods full of ducks this morning? I've counted eleven mallards and mates, including three on the pond. The gentle song of a willow warbler, thank goodness – I was becoming concerned. But what on earth is *that* noise? That rattling bark. Ah – I'm under a raven tree, the vast bird is right above me: what a fearsome, primitive percussion.

A goshawk has been sighted in the Gorge: this is immensely exciting because they are the most reckless of hunters, flinging themselves through brambles after their prey, and apparently their eyes can glow like fire: *a glare of goshawks*.

12th April

Bird of the day

A blackbird swoops over the blue like a swallow over water

This is the first morning I've *smelled* the bluebells: they need to be nearly full-flowered for this. In the distance, a blackbird swoops over the blue like a swallow over water.

Wood Sorrel

Woodland blackbirds differ from the blackbirds we enjoy in our gardens: here they're elusive, alarmist and clucky, and far less tolerant of human proximity.

One day I'll compile a shade card of wood violets; there's such a range of blues from wisps of sky to deepest royal purple.

The great tit is my woodland bird of the day – the chest markings dramatically dark now, and the birds themselves seem to have doubled in size ... And what a dizzying whirr the goldcrests are making – there are six with me in this yew, their calls as thin and sharp as pine needles.

First contact

We looked into each other's eyes

Everything changed this morning. My time was short – time enough to get to the raven tree but not to where the goshawk might be (I now say *the* goshawk rather than the more speculative *a* goshawk).

I walked in the slow toe-to-heel way we practise in my gym balance class. The dawn was luminous: only Heaven could be more beautiful. On the path ahead, but close, too close – a doe. She froze, huge ears erect. I stood still, my legs slightly apart like hers, hands to my sides. We looked into each other's eyes. Minutes passed. The deer tilted her head to one side and so did I. She moved towards me, three steps and she stopped. She bent to scratch her nose with a hoof, straightened and took two more steps forward. Then she turned and picked her way down the slope.

As I moved on there was no protest from the jays, no mid-song silences from the blackcaps, and the song thrush sung his exquisite solo while I watched his beak open in song. The ravens rattled at each other when I passed below their tree. Willow warblers sung – and great tits flirted and touched beaks in front of me.

Today I'm just part of the business of the woods.

19th April

Playground

Look, don't miss this one ...

Here I am again, first into the woods on the same path, hoping to meet my deer. There's a buck ahead and he's bounding off – so that's the end of that this morning. No, no it *isn't,* there's another deer by the path, half hidden by the yew. It's my doe and she's looking at me again with tilted head curiosity. Now she's following the male, and taking her time, not afraid.

I'm in the playground of four great spotted woodpeckers – each pair keeping distance from the other, chasing through the ash trees around this bluebell clearing.
Now here are two long-tailed tits swinging on the thinnest of branches.

Sometimes the sun highlights a single bluebell or violet, as though it's saying, *Look, don't miss this one ...*

The leaves of this wood sorrel are polka-dotted with silver rain.

This morning, the paths are spongy with mud and pitted with animal tracks. I can follow the night movements of the foxes, the badgers and the deer: it's my way of walking with them.

20th April

Collision (a fragment)

I was walking too fast, preoccupied, not expecting the doe to be on this part of the path. We almost collided and she bounded away.

23rd April

Handel

I'm not hiding anymore

This isn't *my* doe. It's another and I've caught her unawares, grazing on the plain. I freeze. She waits, and then starts to walk towards me, little by little. My heart is

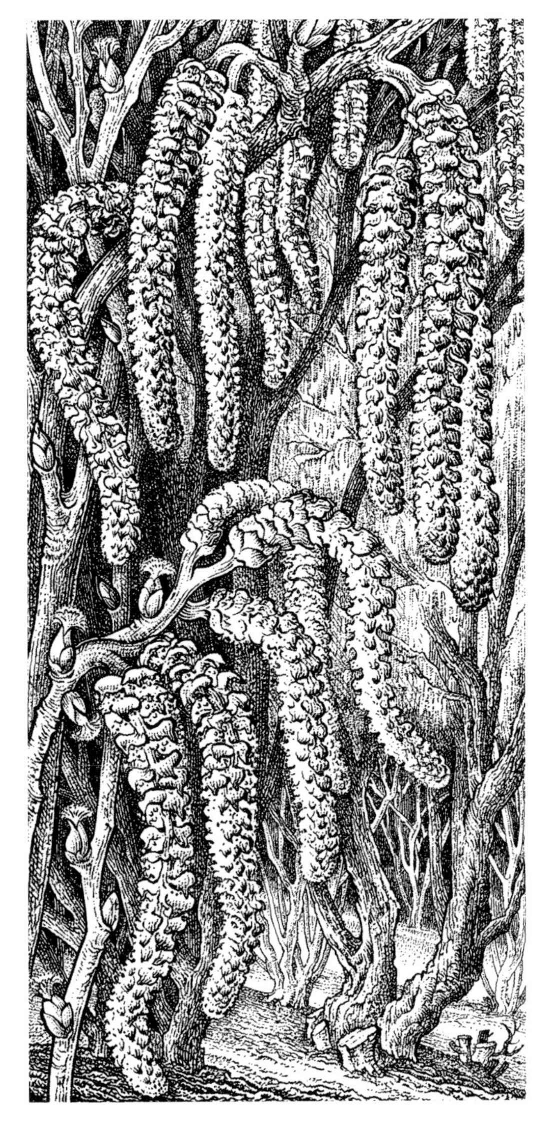

Hazel

thudding so much that I want her to run away, but she doesn't. She starts to graze again, and I walk on. They know I'm here, the birds and animals. I'm not hiding, just walking with hands in pockets and singing. Handel's *I know that my redeemer liveth* is perfectly paced for bird watching and I hope that the birds will take this as my song, my species call. I pass under an ash inhabited by a hysterical green woodpecker and I stop. This time it *is* my doe and she's seen me. I tilt my head and she walks four steps forwards.

The buck appears and they both stare at me, then, like the first doe, they start to graze, looking up from time to time.

Stones moving about …

A world without writing

There was a lull in birdsong this morning, a flagging of energy. I began to sing the *Hallelujah Chorus*. Instantly, birds started to sing again, chiffchaff, song thrush, blackcap!

Now I'm sitting on a big stone under a yew that is one of a semi-circle of ancient yews. I'm near a twelve-hole badger sett, and deer and badgers have patterned the mud of the paths: I'm sure squirrels have crossed also, but they are too light for footprints. I can hear goldcrests and blue tits in the yews and a song thrush is operatic in the nearby beech. The woodland floor is inky with bluebells.

On my sitting stone are the professionally carved words:

AND STONES MOVED SILENTLY ACROSS THE WORLD

I guess this is about inspiring awe although it's partly about being unable to allow a world without writing. If we learn the language of the woods there's plot, character, music, drama, menace, danger, poetry, ethics, philosophy and awe enough to grip the mind for ever: writing is a poor substitute. On the other hand, if the words on the stone inspired this thought, then they've worked magic.

The doe was alone on the path this morning and actually started to trot towards me. She was so close, stopped, and then ambled down the Gorge. She's poignantly beautiful and, unless I'm deceiving myself, I don't want to tame her, as that would put her in danger. This is about something else; this is about my longing to be wild.

29th April

A serious situation with a wren

Mindful of the outraged blackcap, I apologise and retreat

The woods feel edgy this morning: we had thunder and lightning overnight but there's more to it than that. Today is part of a bank holiday weekend and the woods have been full of people: it'll be several days before wildlife ranges openly again.

A great spotted woodpecker surfs away with an exasperated yelp and there are no deer on the path. No, wait, there's the doe in the undergrowth, peeping out. I walk past in slow motion, my heart thudding, but I hear her rushing down the slope.

I am counting the holes in this badger sett: goodness knows *why* I am counting them – perhaps auditing is a human instinct or something from childhood – *Look at the ducks, how many can you count? How many sheep? How many little lambs?* A wren leaves the ivy to wag his tail and shout at me face to face. This is serious: usually this wren bursts into song as I walk past, singing.

Mindful of the outraged blackcap, I apologise and retreat and it's then that I see the female wren with a little white feather in her beak, obviously intent on lining her nest, weaving in and out of ash roots exposed by badger diggings, finally slipping into a tiny crease in a tree stump.

More thunder and lightning and the chiffchaff and song thrush sing louder to match the noise. Two swifts slice the sky. I can hear the harsh, open-ended shrieks of a goshawk (I've been learning it from the internet, playing it over and over until it echoes in my head). Two herons sail into the clouds, there's a sudden wind and large drops of water fall on my notebook.

Could there ever be a scent to match bluebells in the rain? Fantastic, *fantastic …*

Lily-of-the-valley

When my late father was elderly, he made nightly rounds of his property, full of wartime spirit, ready to challenge any unknown noise or light. Once, he encountered glow-worms at the bottom of his orchard and he telephoned me to tell me *so much light from a little insect – like little torches! Fantastic! Fantastic!*

May 1st

Passion

This is what I believe

Rain has set in. The woods are dark but lively because rain-drops patter on the woodland floor and rattle the leaves in an illusion of voles scuttling and small birds landing. There's not a full complement of birdsong, but the chiffchaff and blackcap are making valiant efforts.

The rain has penetrated my plastic mac and I shelter under a yew. My glasses steam up in the tree's warmth and I've nothing dry to clear them with. Also, I can't stay here all morning; I've got to go to work. I trek on, slip and fall in puddle: I'm now brown with mud. I wash my hands in the puddle but I feel low, cold and wet, a long way from home and obliged to question what I am doing here.

It's a passion, people say, *you have a passion. Where does it come from?* Well, this much I know: my mum was paralysed, and even now my every step outside is a miracle. In spirit I take her to see what for half of her life she loved in memory. *I'd give anything,* she used to say, *just to walk in the rain.*

My beloved son's here, too. When he flew as a falcon, he left his robin spirit in the woods, as it was when we three explored them as a young family. We've been together in these woods for a precious fragment of eternity. Peter's forever here searching for badgers and orchids and hearing the willow warbler, hugging me in excitement and whispering *fantastic, fantastic* ...

Then, I'm often asked, *don't you feel afraid alone in the woods*? This is a reflection of the fear of the enquirer, of course, and an expression of care for me, which I partly appreciate but mostly dread because each time I must suppress a plea for understanding: *This is who I am, this is what I do, and even if I were afraid I would do it anyway because I wouldn't want to go on living if I couldn't.*

I find staying indoors for any length of time more alarming than being in woods. I'm wary of indoor emotions but there's such renewal here that my hopes rise, and hard memories reconcile. Walking in this playground of grace, it would be perverse not to resolve to live generously. This is where I learn to get on with things.

I need to remember that when I'm as wet and wretched as now.

Wren and Primroses

Also, I'm not here to get away from people, I'm here to do what I feel is the best part of being human and then I'll be less afraid of what life wants from me. I've been finding the meaning of life in woods since childhood and I'm astonished that folk can get through the day without seeing what I see.

But for those who envy my passion, this is what I believe: given an interest, passion can follow. If it's wildlife, visit an area regularly until it becomes a habit. Habit leads to appetite, and appetite becomes passion if the interest and caring are there: as a therapist, I try to make a relationship with everything I see.

Go to your wildlife place often, and there will come a time when you care deeply about individual violets, the wrens, the colour of the beech leaves. Continue to do it when others sense there's something odd about you and it isn't comfortable. They'll honour your passion even though they are wary of it and may not want to hear, but this won't matter.

Do it because by then you'll know important things about our planet, you'll know that even on a sullen, bird-silent, July morning when the woods are exhausted and the winds are sighs, even then the scent of wild honeysuckle from some secret place in the dark-leaved trees is part of the promise of Heaven.

And I write because I'd burst if I didn't: writing is how I bear the beauty of it; it'd be too much for me otherwise.

I'm trudging home across the Clifton suspension bridge and what's that big bird flapping slowly like a gull, circling over the valley where I heard that distinctive shriek ... Oh, my goodness, it's so close that I can see the outline of its head. Here I am, soaking wet, muddy, cold, almost lonely, and I'm seeing my first goshawk ...

Contest

What fickleness, what abandonment!

I'm craving to see the goshawk again. But am I simply worshipping another celebrity? Has this replaced my longing to see the doe? The song *Clementine* has always tormented me – those lines, *so I kissed her little sister and forgot my Clementine*. What fickleness! What abandonment!

Once, there was an acre of wild lily of the valley in this wood, an area (still) called Lily Point although most of it was quarried out of existence. The lilies are flourishing again, brave butterfly leaves poised on the edge of the Gorge.

Oh, this operatic duet! A song thrush and a blackbird singing passionately to assert their territories, neither bird waiting for the other to pause, each drowning the other in song. And their ash trees are so close together that the branches are holding hands.

The fragrance of bluebells is coming to me on a cold wind.

Moon music, and battle cries

Without birdsong, it's harder to keep my concerns at bay

Something's changed – fewer birds are singing: now they're shadows fluttering in the cover. Nesting, not singing is the birds' priority and this, I think, marks the shift from spring to summer.

Without birdsong, it's harder to keep my concerns at bay. Walking the path, deep in thought, I nearly collide with the doe's bottom. She jumps, turns, sees me, hesitates and is off. Not particularly satisfactory, as encounters go.

I watch a lipstick-breasted bullfinch slip into the ivy around a tree stump, and I pick a pretty grey feather from the side of the path. I rub the feather against my cheeks, and then replace it so that a wren can gather it for her nest.

It's that song thrush again, the one that battled the blackbird. His phrases are mostly upbeat, some raucous, others cheeky, but every few minutes, he selects a six-note descending phrase and repeats this just twice: a waterfall of sound, as silver as the moon. I reflect that birds were the first musicians in our universe and I stay under the ash until those notes come again.

I'm now sitting under the yew on the *stones moving silently* slab, thankful that the stone is keeping still while I write my notes. And what's that? The nastiest battle cries I have heard in the woods, so doubtless a jay is implicated. Through binoculars, I see a raven and a jay slugging it out in the canopy, hurling threats and oaths. The jay pursues the raven out of sight and in the quiet beneath the jay's ash, I hear a repeated purring – probably the female jay on the nest.

On my way home, I stop in a clearing to inhale bluebells and a goshawk unfolds from the ground like the phantom of the woods.

Conversation with a deer

Only temporarily seduced by the goshawk

Something extraordinary has happened. The woods were vibrant with frosty light today, the emerald beeches enamelled and buttercups shining little suns below them. I was hoping for another goshawk sighting and wasn't prepared to encounter my doe, reposed in the sunlight by the path.

Why wasn't she standing up and moving away? Was she injured? Abandoned? It took a few seconds to sink in that she wasn't moving because she didn't see any need to.

Common Violet

We were six feet apart and she was as beautiful as a fairy tale. My heart was thumping and I started to talk, silly endearments as I would to my rabbit; then, encouraged by her attention (one of her ears rotated slightly in my direction), I told her about my book of woodland tales, and how she was in it and how I was only *temporarily* seduced by the goshawk...

This had obviously all gone too far for her mate who, unknown to me, was lolling about, eavesdropping behind a fallen tree trunk. He rolled and heaved to his feet and so, more delicately, did she. They wandered off, but she looked back.

The scientist in me knows that this relationship is about habituation and curiosity rather than rapport. But as a woodlander, I'm happy that I was able to tell her about this book and the goshawk. I'm glad she knows.

Life in the bush 29 May 6.30 am

Hold back and hope ...

OK, what's all this? What's going on? This great spotted woodpecker is flying in circles and yelping. Something's wrong. Also, impaled on a low twig of this oak, I find a crumpled map of the woods and an invitation to a party *on the ancient fort ...*

Years ago, when the woods were wilder and not as beautiful, I was a voluntary warden here with a badge, armbands, and authority to challenge. I'm simply a woodlander now, content to hold back and hope. So when I pass a cluster of tents below the bank of the fort, and a young girl raises her hand in greeting, I raise mine in return and make no mention of *camping being forbidden or not asking permission …*

Later, I find three youngsters at the entrance to the woods, and several more struggling down the path with black rubbish sacks. There's a girl and boy sitting in an open car boot and they smile at me.

Were you here all night? I ask, *what was it like? What did you see?*
This unlocks a tumbling of words, a waterfall of wonder.
It was – it was incredible – the sun was this golden disc, and there was all this red, pollution red … but maybe not – and everything went orange, all our faces … we climbed up to the top of the camp – never seen anything so amazing …
They begin an intense debate as to whether the birds started to sing before or after the rising of the golden disc.
I ask, *did you see any deer?*
Are there DEER here?
Yes, but I expect they're engaged in family carryings on ...
Does that mean there will be BAMBIS? Asks the young man
I've got to see them …
Did you see badgers?
There are BADGERS here?

If I saw a badger I'd want to make friends with it. I told you life in the bush was great, says the girl to the young man, *I told you ...*
Listen, she says to me, *you have to come here early and see it, get out of your bed, come over here at five and see it all. You have to ...*

She clasps arms with me for a moment, and I walk away from these youngsters, themselves as golden as deer and as compelling of my tenderness and respect.

Postscript

Mesmerised by the impossibility of what was happening ...

Birds, deer, squirrels, foxes, furry scuttlers (bank voles et al), they all *know* I'm in the woods. I hide in plain sight and don't attempt to deceive. I want them to see me, predict my movements and get the measure of me.

My visits are regular, every few days, every day when I can. I go at the same time, and get anxious if I'm late. I need to be turning the corners at exactly the same moment. In return, I see the same birds on the same branches, singing the same songs, not breaking off as I pass.

Recently, Jean, my cousin, wrote that her blackbird in Somerset starts his morning song at 4.15. On the day after I received her letter, I was awake and ready to check the starting time of our garden blackbird: 4.15 almost to the

The Woodland in Spring

second. Wildlife hears a different drumbeat; I need to act as though I hear it, too.

I tread the same route at the same pace, hands in pockets, rarely stopping. When you are next in woodland, or in a country lane listening to birds, notice how they cease singing when you stop walking, and start again once you do.

My own singing, my repeated species call, is activated by light – I sing in light areas and fall silent in the shade and in the rain. I sing most when the sun is out and this pattern seems to fall in with the human spirit.

Woodland blackbirds are beginning to accept my presence; this matters because the alarm of one blackbird is taken up by another and then another and whole areas are rapidly alerted. Early this year, I walked through widening shockwaves of blackbird alarm, caused by a skirmishing magpie. The bullet-like squawks jarred me; I lost my balance and fell. Is this what bird alarm calls do – disrupt the focus and movement of the attacker?

Alarm calls are serious. They're often a desperate attempt to protect their nest and fledglings. It's the instinct to protect, to repel boarders, it's the Battle of Britain, it's Custer's last stand ... If you suspect that it's your presence causing distress, do as I do, apologise and walk on quickly.

Once I had the fantasy that I was a hunter, focused, disregarding anything irrelevant, locked onto my target.

My targets then were rare flowers, especially orchids, and I've been good at it.

Now my fantasy is to be a twenty-first century woodlander and *everything* is relevant. Why the change? Being a rare plant hunter is wildly satisfying, make no mistake, it gives life an immense electricity and structure. But it blinkers the nature of adventure and experience.

Now, I walk the woods slowly, open to whatever comes my way, searching for nothing in particular. Yet come my way spectacular adventures do. Today (mid June), I paused briefly to smell wild honeysuckle, and then wheeled round to face what looked and sounded like a cavalry charge. Hurtling directly towards me across a vast, felled area were two deer, led by the doe. Deer charging *towards* me? An *attack*? *Roe deer* on the rampage? I was too mesmerised by the impossibility of what was happening to take evasive action.

They were on me, the doe passed just outside touching distance and I stepped back. That careless movement was enough to deter the buck – he froze, and then raced back the way he had come. Whatever that was about, I'll never know. Maybe something frightened them back in the woods and bolting towards me was the less alarming option: but thinking about it, perhaps it was a courtship chase.

As a hunter, I knew what I would find, what my adventure would be: as a woodlander, I don't. When I started to write these accounts of my early mornings in the woods, I had no idea that such an astonishing story would unfold.

The story goes on . . .

Turn the page and follow Geraldine through the year on her tour of Echo lands in each edition of Eye On Local Nature Magazine.

ECHO LANDS is the first EYE ON book.

EYE ON LOCAL NATURE magazine began in 1982 as a venture between two Bristol primary school boys, Peter Taylor and Matt Jones. This unique magazine flourished, is read nationally and internationally, and is now published by the EYE ON team – Peter, Geraldine & Keith Taylor.

As a result of the magazine, the acclaimed artist Robin Tanner and his wife Heather offered their friendship and patronage, as have dozens of other wildlife experts and enthusiasts. EYE ON LOCAL NATURE retains its community base, publishing observations about the bird, insect, animal and plant life seen in local environments.

Follow Geraldine through the year on her tour of Echo lands in each edition of EYE ON LOCAL NATURE magazine.

- -

Eye On is published quarterly and costs £3.00 for 4 issues including postage.

Please send a cheque for £3.00 made payable to:
Geraldine Taylor – 28, Berkeley Road, Westbury Park, Bristol BS6 7PJ.

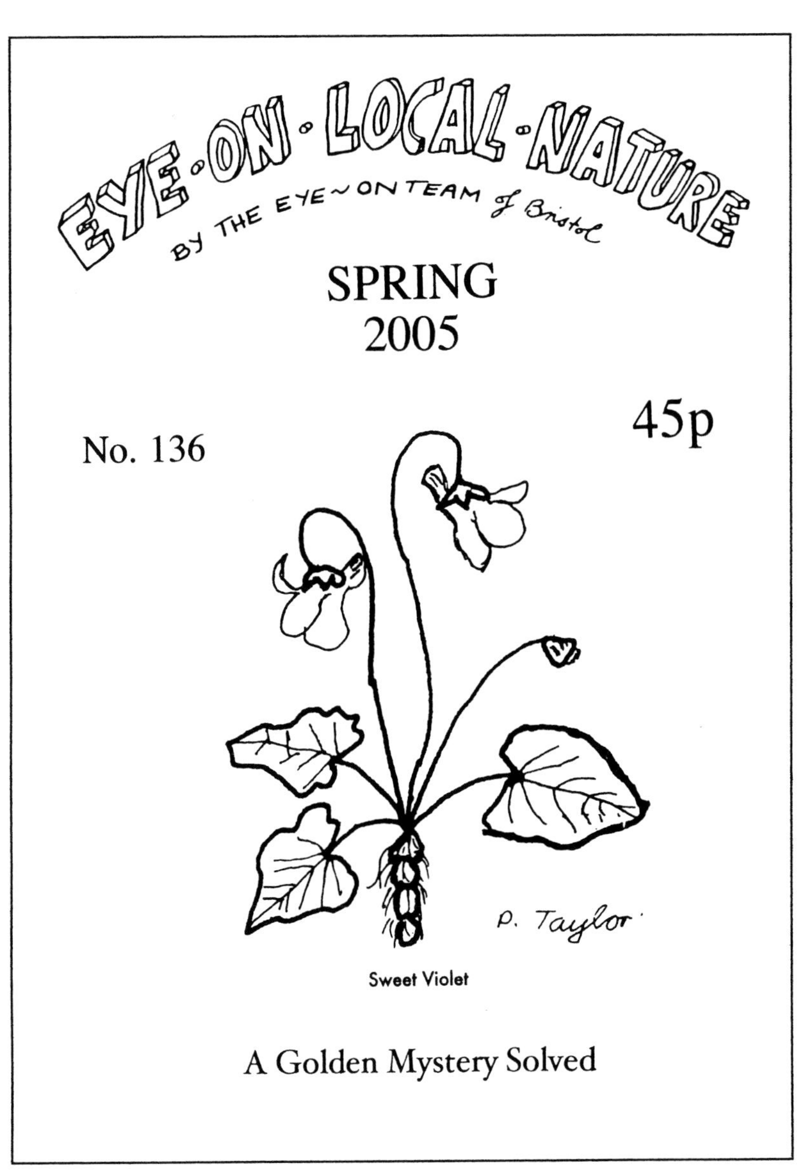

Actual size of magazine 210mm x 150mm